Charles M. Schulz

Your Dog Plays Hockey?

HarperFestival®

A Division of HarperCollinsPublishers

A Packaged Goods Incorporated Book. Copyright © 1996 by United Feature Syndicate, Inc. PEANUTS © United Feature Syndicate, Inc. Based on the PEANUTS® comic strip by Charles M. Schulz. Printed in Hong Kong. All rights reserved.

"Your stupid dog is in the emergency room at the hospital!"

"Good grief!"

"My poor dog! I wonder what happened to him. It's terrible to be lying in the emergency room all by yourself! I wonder what he's thinking right now..."

"Yes, Ma'am, I'm here to see my dog...is he all right? He got hurt playing hockey? I wonder how it happened..."

"It's hard to talk to someone who keeps fainting all the time."

"Hello? This is Marcie. May I speak to Charles, please?"

"He just called from the hospital. His stupid dog hurt himself playing hockey. What's a dog doing playing hockey?"

"My Grampa is sixty-five and he plays hockey."

"He must be some beagle!"

I was playing hockey,
Wayne Gretzky tripped me!

She looked like Wayne Gretzky.

"They're coming to get you for your knee surgery. Don't be afraid...in a few weeks you'll be as good as ever."

"Marcie! What are you doing here?"

"I heard your dog was having surgery so I thought you'd like to have someone sit with you. We could have a cup of hot chocolate, but the machine is out of order."

"Hospital waiting rooms
are designed this way."

"I think you should ask the nurse, Charles. It's your dog who's having the surgery. Go ahead, ask her."

"Ma'am? Do dogs have knees? What I want to know, Ma'am, is how can they do knee surgery on my dog if dogs don't have knees? You didn't know he was a dog?! Well, could you call down to surgery right away? Thank you."

"She said they thought he was a little kid with a big nose!"

"Thank you, Ma'am.
We appreciate it."

"They've canceled Snoopy's knee surgery."

"Did they say why?"